P~~raise for~~

WORDS' WORTH
Vocabulary Verse

Word-verses, 52 of them, going up the alphabet and back down. 52 weeks in the year. This little book could be used as a weekly almanac. Trouble is, bet you can't read just one per week! *-Belle Leddurs*

I especially enjoyed the quotations from literature that describe words in general and that show the featured word in context. *- Wanda Full*

No **vacillating** here. The decision is quick and unanimous. WORDS'WORTH is a great read. Learning new words or seeing familiar ones by way of light verse is the ticket. *-A.D. Light*

How to describe this book? How about **cockamamie insouciance**? And I'm not just **bamboozling**! *-S.N. Schull*

Susan Jones, aka WORDS'WORTH, has produced a gem, a literary flourish (flounce, **furbelow**). She has "let flie," with delightful and amusing results. *-Eddy Torreal*

Mrs. Jones has given us a "livre juste" filled with **mots justes**. A treat to read. *-Bob Lew*

WORDS'WORTH is a refreshing **zephyr**, an **umbrageous** retreat. Or should I say *Treat, Re-Treat.* *- E.Z. Reed*

Find the nearest **tuffet**, sit back, and enjoy this **gallimaufry** of delights. *-Frank Lee Grayt*

Get your **quotidian** dose of WORDS'WORTH. This is one unique, **hunky-dory** tome. *-A. Mused*

No need for **susurrus** here. This is a book worth shouting about. *-A. Djem*

Fun, instructive, highly amusing, intelligent, and nicely presented. Oh, and I loved the word selections and verses, too. *-Shirley Fein*

A thoroughly enjoyable walk through the alphabet. *-X.M. Plurry*

I almost had forgotten
That words were meant for rhyme:
And yet how well I knew it –
Once upon a time!

Christopher Morley (1890-1957)

What is WORDS'WORTH©?

WORDS'WORTH is a spotlight on WORDS – old and new, familiar and unusual, domestic and foreign – combining rhyme, and quotations, and whimsy! It is a way for young and old to have fun with language.

In short, WORDS'WORTH is vocabulary verse.

Each WORDS'WORTH features a vocabulary word with pronunciation, definitions, and related words. And each includes at least one relevant quotation that uses the featured word in its text. There are also "word" quotations included – quotes that are actually about words – but that also relate to the meaning of the featured word and verse. Finally, there is a verse composed specifically for the word.

WORDS'WORTH grew from a request by fellow workers of their corporate librarian in a Midwestern insurance company. They wanted a weekly vocabulary word via the company e-mail. This led to searches for appropriate, unusual words – keeping eyes and ears open for likely "candidates" – in the news, in quotation books, in professional and recreational reading. Many times, literature and humorous verse provided the weekly words. Often, these sources suggested or prompted a response, also using the selected word.

And so, WORDS'WORTH was born.

When I feel inclined to read poetry, I take down my dictionary. The poetry of words is quite as beautiful as the poetry of sentences.

Oliver Wendell Holmes (1809-1894)

Words' Worth's

Vocabulary Verse

A to Z

and Back Again

All words are pegs to hang ideas on.

Henry Ward Beecher (1813-1887)

Words' Worth's

Vocabulary Verse

A to Z

and Back Again

A Rhyming Romp through the Alphabet

Susan Jones

Whimsy Publishing
Publications for the Well-Versed
Tilghman Island, MD

WORDS'WORTH'S VOCABULARY VERSE A TO Z AND BACK AGAIN

Whimsy Publishing, www.whimsypublishing.com
PO Box 296, Tilghman Island, MD 21671, U.S.A.
orders@whimsypublishing.com

Copyright © 2010 by Susan Jones

All rights reserved. No part of this book may be reproduced or transmitted in any form or by any means, electronic or mechanical, including photocopying, recording, or by any information storage and retrieval system, without written permission from the author, except for the inclusion of brief quotations in a review.

Quotation with jabot (Ellen Tien) used with permission from the *New York Times* www.nytimes.com.
Quotation with jabot (Jerry Brewer) used with permission from the *Seattle Times* www.seattletimes.com
Quotation with rodomontade (Nicholas Barber) used with permission from *The Independent* www.independent.co.uk/.
Quotation with nimiety used with permission from the Sunday Star-Times (New Zealand) http://www.stuff.co.nz/sunday-star-times
Quotation with lissome used with permission from Richard Lederer www.verbivore.com.
Quotation with career/careen (Editorial) used with permission from the *Montreal Gazette* www.montrealgazette.com.

Jones, Susan A.
WORDS'WORTH'S vocabulary verse A to Z and back again : a rhyming romp through the alphabet / Susan Jones.
LCCN: 2010929497
ISBN 978-0-615-38897-7
1. Vocabulary – Humor. 2. Humorous poetry. 3. English language – Dictionaries – Humor.

Table of Contents
Verses for

Quotation attributions begin on page 119.
A pronunciation key is on the next page.

Words do wonderful things. They sound, purr. They can urge, they can wheedle, whip, whine. They can sing, sass, singe. They can churn, check, channelize. ...

Gwendolyn Brooks (1917-2000)

Shown	As in	Shown	As in	Shown	As in
ă	hat, mat	ī	like, hide	oo	boo, flute
ā or ay	day	j	joy, juice	ow	out, now
ah or ŏ	hot, lot	k	kit, cat	sh	ship-shape
ai	hair	l	lulu, lad	th	thing, think
ě or eh	pet, men	ng	sing	ŭ or uh	run, hunt
ee	meet	ŏ or ah	not, spot	ur	hurt, birth
ĭ or ih	hit, kiss	ō or oh	hope	zh	Asia

Also, a double consonant following a vowel shortens the vowel.
(E.g. att = hat, mat)

Dedicated to the memory of my parents:

Oline (Lena) Tidslevold Anderson,
who would always take time to read my favorite rhymes,

and

Oscar Adolph Anderson,
who, even at the age of ninety, could recite
"The Walrus and the Carpenter."

A word is dead
When it is said,
Some say.
I say it just
Begins to live
That day.

Emily Dickinson (1830-1886)

Welcome, reader.

I offer you verses. Each features a word,
pronounced and defined; fortified
with quotations that highlight. Sublime to absurd,
there are verbaceous treasures inside.

Each verse is connected with narrative patter
that leads one choice word to the next.
Up the alphabet. Down again. There's laughing matter
and whimsy in this petite text.

So . . .

If you've hunted for words, but in all the wrong places,
if you'd like to find something unique –
a glossary matchless, a verbal oasis,
a lexicon *trés magnifique* –

If you enjoy words, rhyme, and well-crafted phrases,
and like spicing your speech with *français;*
And if humorous verse wins your favor and praises,
and if quotes are your cup of Earl Grey;

And you'd like to blend all the above, in a potion
of magical lexical cheer –
Well, I'm happy to say this is more than a notion.
It's happened. It's WORDS'WORTH. It's here.

Enjoy!

ab ovo

First page, first sentence.
The beginning, right?
And what better place to begin than at the beginning.

William Makepeace Thackeray (1811-1863), in his novel *Philip*, has the line:

> Shall we begin ab ovo, sir?

---
ab ovo, adverb (ahb **ō'** vō)
From the beginning.
A Latin phrase meaning from the egg.
Hence the phrase from the Roman poet Horace, "ab ovo usque ad mala," meaning from the egg to the apples, and alluding to the tradition of starting a meal with eggs and finishing it with apples.

D. H. Lawrence (1885-1930) wrote in *Mornings in Mexico*:

> Is it possible that we are so absolutely, so innocently, so ab ovo ridiculous?

Ab ovo. The beginning. John Simon (b. 1925), in *Paradigms Lost,* wrote:

> In the beginning was the word. But by the time the second word was added to it, there was trouble. For with it came syntax …

The beginning. Forget syntax.
Here's the real trouble: What – or where – is the beginning, anyway?

What comes first – the ovo or the chicken?
It's not always obvious. For example:

ab ovo

I've a tale to relate, but it's up for debate

As to how in the world to commence:

With my hero's demise? Or senescence leastwise,

And a flashback or two for suspense?

With some pivotal deed? Or is there a need

For a masterful building of plot,

And for scenes and tableaus, with my hero in throes,

Torn apart, anguished, tortured, distraught?

From the standpoint of art, would it make sense to start

With an ominous portent of old,

Showing shadows once cast in some primeval past

Yet afflicting our hero's doomed soul?

Should I start with his prime, and then hint at the crime

That suffuses his saga forlorn?

Should this tale Byzantine show him first as a teen?

Or **ab ovo**, the day he was born? 2003

brummagem

Speaking of beginnings, let me explain that beginnings, or etymology, has never been the focus of WORDS'WORTH. My eyes tend to glaze over at lengthy lineages. Such exercises don't seem to help me remember the word, anyway. So I focus instead on using the word in the context of quotations and verse.

However, I always take a quick look at the history or at the root word or most closely related word, and I often get that *aperçu,* that satisfying "Ah, so that's what it's related to" feeling.

Often, there are instances when I find that the etymology does indeed make for an integral presentation of a word and is interesting as well.

Here's an example. In Shakespeare's time, the city of Birmingham was known for making counterfeit coins. With time, the name of the city itself became synonymous with things counterfeit, cheap, or inferior. The pronunciation changed, degenerated, and "dialect-ized" too, until today we have

---

brummagem (**brŭm'** uh jŭm)
It can be an adjective or a noun and is sometimes capitalized, especially in British English.
It means something cheap or inferior, such as tinsel.
As an adjective: showy, gaudy, tawdrily attractive.
As words can be sometimes!

Words may be counterfeit, false coined, and current only from the tongue, without the mind; but passion is in the soul, and always speaks the heart.
Thomas Southern, (1660-1746)

Here are some counterfeit words:

16

brummagem

Tinsel and trinkets and gewgaws and gimcracks;
Baubles and bagatelles, bric-a-brac, knick-knacks;
Synonyms – these are a few, only some –
For brummagem, brummagem, brummagem, jum.

Frippery, furbelows, falderal, frills;
Tawdry and trifles and three-dollar bills;
Spangles and sequins until kingdom come:
Brummagem, brummagem, brummagem, jum.

Counterfeit, trumpery, glitz all for show;
Doodads, and dubious finery faux;
Toss them together, and see them become
Brummagem, brummagem, brummagem, jum. 2003

cockamamie

Counterfeit. Sincere. Hurtful. Soothing. The types and descriptions of words are endless.

The character Jo, in Louisa May Alcott's (1832-1888) *Little Women*, declared:

> I like good strong words, that mean something.

There's something to be said for that.

I think this next word is both a good and a strong word. And it certainly means something. It's fortunate that I'm not overly concerned about word origins, since most dictionaries don't say too much about the derivation of this one.

---

cockamamie, adj. (**kŏk'** uh may mee)
(Also spelled cockamamy, as in our example below.)
Ludicrous; nonsensical, as a cockamamie reason for not completing an assignment or going to work.
Perhaps an alteration of decalcomania (a paper transfer), according to the *American Heritage Dictionary of the English Language, 4th Edition.*

In the movie *In the Line of Fire*, Clint Eastwood says to his partner, Dylan McDermott:

> Cockamamy, that's a … that's a word your generation hasn't embraced yet. Maybe you ought to use it once in a while, just to kind of keep it alive, you know.

I'm doing my best to keep it alive via verse … you know!

cockamamie

Words just slay me. **Cockamamie**,
For example. What a gem!
To convey *absurdité*, it's
Sans pareil. Crème de la crème.

Asinine expresses fine a
Sense of the ridiculous;
And moronic's "synonomic."
So is foolish, if you must!

Tomfool, lame-brained, idiotic –
Periodic use is neat.
But to best express illogic,
Cockamamie can't be beat! 1999

disingenuous

Louisa May Alcott's Jo argued for good, strong, meaningful words.

Writer and poet Dorothy Parker (1893-1967) took a different approach in these lines from "The Lady's Reward":

> Keep your pretty words serene;
> Never murmur what you mean.
> Show yourself, by word and look,
> Swift and shallow as a brook.

Swift and shallow, pretty, serene.

One evening several years ago, I was sitting in my kitchen. I had the radio tuned to a public radio station, which was doing one of its interminable fund drives. The focus was on Judy Collins – interviews interspersed with some of her recordings. One of her featured pieces was "I'll Learn to Love the Fallow Way."

I've known many people who love the "shallow" way. They're

---

disingenuous, adj. (dĭs' ĭn **jĕn'** yoo ŭs)
Lacking in candor or straightforwardness.
Giving a false appearance of simple frankness.

Jane Austen (1775-1817) has this line in *Persuasion*:

> My line of conduct will be more direct. Mr. Elliot is evidently a disingenuous, artificial, worldly man, who has never had any better principle to guide him than selfishness.

I thought of some of these people whom I've known, and I thought of Dorothy Parker's words. I substituted "shallow" for "fallow," changed the tense, and created the following verse.

disingenuous

I've learned to love the shallow way;
To mince my words, embrace cliché,
And prattle on *avec plaisir,*
Eschewing depth for thin veneer.

I've learned to use the guarded phrase.
Impassioned language nowadays
Is such an impropriety
In mealy-mouthed society.
I'm tossing candor down the sink.
I'm **disingenuous**. (I think!)

I've learned to love the shallow way.
Profundity seems so passé.
I've grown accustomed to the trite,
And superficial seems just right.

I feign an interest insincere;
I'm not concerned, but "Oh my dear,"
I smile, and nod, and seem intent;
But what I said's not what I meant.
I'm not the friend I seem to be;
I'm **disingenuous**, you see. 2000

eructation

Being disingenuous can get us into trouble of Shakespeare's tangled-web variety. Some of us just can't master the skill of watching our words, controlling our tongues, and keeping our stories straight. This may lead to another consequence, too.

We may have to eat our words. Even Winston Churchill admitted to having been in that predicament. Whereas this situation may cause some of us chagrin or awkwardness, Churchill maintained, "Eating words has never given me indigestion."

Indigestion. Sometimes, in a social situation, the results can seem – if not disastrous – at least embarrassing.

Tobias Smollett (1721-1771) wrote in *Don Quixote*, "Beware … of chewing on both sides of your mouth, as well as eructing before company."

John Evelyn, in *Aceteria* (1699), wrote, "Cabbage is greatly accus'd for lying undigested in the Stomack and provoking Eructations."

Beware of what? Provoking what?

Walt Whitman (1819-1892) gives a clue:

> The sound of the belch'd words of my voice loos'd to the eddies of the wind.

---

eructation, noun (ih rŭk **tay'** shŭn)
The act of belching; the voiding of wind from the stomach through the mouth; a belch or burp.
Verb, eruct, to belch. Adjective, eructative.

The poet Henry More (1614-1687) admitted, "Oft the soul lets flie such unexpected eructations."

My soul "let flie," too, and the resulting verse is opposite.

eructation

Important social situations

Can be spoiled by **eructations** –

Those airy outbursts one must squelch –

From indigestion's fruits … a belch!

So, take small bites. Don't gulp. Don't slurp.

And stifle (need I say?) that burp.

Should nature win? You're ill at ease?

Say, "'Scuse my **eructation**, please."   1999

flout

Of course, the preceding advice is of concern only to those who care about manners, convention and social approbation.

What about those who never met a rule they didn't enjoy breaking?

We might call them lovers of freedom. (Freedom for themselves, anyway!)

And as freedom lovers, perhaps they're also natural-born poets, if we stretch the reasoning of writer, philosopher, and scholar Norman O. Brown (1913-2002):

> Freedom is poetry, taking liberties with words, breaking the rules of normal speech, violating common sense.

Here's a word for freedom lovers and for spurners of rules in general:

---

flout, verb (flowt)
To show scorn or contempt, e.g. to flout a law.
To treat with contemptuous disregard.
Not to be confused with **flaunt** – to show off, brandish, display ostentatiously.

There seems to be the view, particularly among writers, that poetry exemplifies the finest instances of rule-breaking, and that this somehow equates with freedom and truth.

For what it's worth, H.L. Mencken (1880-1956) wrote in *Smart Set,* June 1920:

> Its (poetry's) essential character lies in its bold flouting of what every reflective adult knows to be the truth.

I've written a little verse for the flouters of the world.

flout

I've written this ditty to call your attention
To my absolute scorn and disdain for convention.
Conformity? Customs? Compliance? Decorum?
I don't give a hoot; and what's more, I abhor 'em!

Complaisance is not in my nature. I spurn
Amenities social. Rules aren't a concern.
Propriety, mores, and manners I **flout**,
With chip on my shoulder, and thumb on my snout. 2003

glabrous

Now, what if that person, whether flouting convention or not, moved his thumb up from his nose to the top of his head? What would he feel?

Words have texture. Grammarian and political columnist James J. Kilpatrick (b. 1920) wrote of the tactile quality of words:

> . . . we find rough words, smooth words, words with splintered edges, words to shout or whisper with, words that caress, words that strike.

Let's assume that our flouter's thumb found a smooth surface on the top of his head. We could call him bald, but why not instead, for variety, try a different word?

---

glabrous, adj. (**glay'** brŭs)
Smooth. Having a surface destitute of hair, down, projections, or pubescence. Bald.
Used frequently in science to describe leaves, fruits, insects, beaks, and the like. For example, you could describe the nectarine as a glabrous peach.

The word is often used humorously to describe baldness, or a clean-shaven face. Oliver Wendell Holmes (1809-1894), in his novel *Elsie Venner*, wrote of :

> … two or three notabilities of Rockland, with geoponic eyes, and glabrous, bumpless foreheads.

In case you're wondering about the "geoponic eyes," Holmes is poking fun there, too, using a word that denotes things agricultural to mean rustic or countrified.

No poking fun here. Just a bit of smooth, bald-faced whimsy:

glabrous

Glabrous? Think babe-rous. (Newborn.)

Youthfully smooth. (Unadorned.)

Nary a hair. (Not a root.)

Crown without down. (Non-hirsute.)

Fully un-woolly. (No fluff.)

Stubble untroubled. (Bare. Buff.)

Matchlessly thatchless. (So called.)

Glabrous? Toupee'd-less. (That's bald.)   2004

 hauteur

We moved up from the nose to the pate. Let's go back to the nose. There are those who thumb their noses. There are also those who elevate theirs. Stick them in the air, so to speak. Act snooty. Some time ago, I came across this Balliol rhyme:

> I am tall and rather stately,
> And I care not very greatly
> What you say or what you do.

I thought I could sense a bit of disdain or arrogance. Haughtiness. I love this quote from Shakespeare's *Henry VI Part I*:

> I am vanquished; these haughty words of hers
> Have batter'd me like roaring cannon-shot.

What better word to express haughtiness than

---

hauteur, noun (hō **toor'** – or ō **toor'**)
French.
Haughtiness in bearing and attitude; arrogance.
Loftiness, disdain, overbearing attitude.

It would be very natural if a certain hauteur, a certain carriage of the head, a certain curl of the lip, distinguished every one whose name is Smith.
G. K. Chesterton (1874-1936), *Heretics*

Or Jones, perhaps. Or – (Substitute any name!)

Here's a verse I wrote back in 2000 about a word with attitude. I titled it "If Nouns Could Speak."

hauteur

If Nouns Could Speak

I'm **hauteur**, noun of discernment.

French extraction. Nose upturn-ment.

Chin raised slightly. Lofty mien.

(Peers are few and far between.)

Bearing regal, carriage lordly.

Snobbish? I go over-boardly!

Proud demeanor. Haughty air.

(Humble? Modest? *Au contraire!*)

My vainglory comes innately;

I'm no *nouveau Jean*-Come-Lately.

Condescending through and through,

I'm **hauteur**. (Do I know you?) 2000

indolence

We just heard from a haughty, proud word (hauteur). As we just read, Shakespeare (1564-1616) wrote of "these haughty words of hers." He also wrote in *The Rape of Lucrece*:

> Out, idle words, servants to shallow fools!
> Unprofitable sounds, weak arbitrators!

Idle words. We've already heard from pride. How about another mortal sin: sloth. Hence Shakespeare's idle words! We're going to call sloth

---

indolence, noun (ĭn' dl ŭns)
The state of being indolent, adj.
Disinclination to exert oneself. Habitual laziness; lethargy, sloth, idleness.

Tyron Edwards (1809-1894) wrote:

> Indolence is the dry rot of even a good mind and a good character; the practical uselessness of both.

William Hazlitt (1778-1830) took a slightly more tolerant view:

> Indolence is a delightful but distressing state; we must be doing something to be happy.

I can relate to the opinion of Bern Williams, who said, "I like the word indolence. It makes my laziness seem classy."

> Turn on the prudent ant thy heedful eyes.
> Observe her labours, sluggard, and be wise.
> Samuel Johnson (1709-1784), based on *Proverbs 6:6*

I turned my heedful eyes inward, and here's my resulting confession:

indolence

This little rhyme might make more sense

But for a thing called **indolence**.

I try to raise my hand and pen,

Then idly put them down again.

I'm tempted by a force intense

To laze – give in to **indolence**,

Delightful yet distressing state

Of languor. I capitulate!

My mind's infested with dry rot;

My character has gone to pot.

What words describe this weary mess?

Well – torpor, sloth, and laziness;

And adjectives like dilatory;

Shiftless, sluggish, sorry story!

Active verbs? Huh uh. They're hazy,

Passive. State-of-being-lazy.

Perhaps next week my attitude

Will have cast off this lassitude.

But now? My listless present tense

Is all wrapped up in **indolence**.   1999

jabot

James Thurber (1894-1961) gave an alternative view when he wrote:

> It is better to have loafed and lost than never to have loafed at all.

I was loafing – indolently, idly, lazily, sluggardly reading the *New York Times* one Sunday, and found this in a fashion article by Ellen Tien, entitled "The Ripple Effect" (October 1, 2006, pg. 9.3):

> This fall, designers are using ruffles as flourishes in varied and lovely ways. Whether in a classic jabot at the throat of a blouse, in micro-rows at the cuff of a sleeve or in one striking ripple down the front of a coat, ruffles are no longer party-girl tacky but are, by turns, racy, elegant, flirtatious and anything but predictable. Fancy that.

---

jabot, noun (zhă **boh'**)
A decorative cascade of ruffles or other arrangement of lace or cloth down the front of a blouse, shirt, or dress.
French – the crop of a bird.

More than a century before, in 1898, the *Daily News* said:

> The jabot has secured a fresh lease of life, and has elongated itself from the neck to the waist.

"Jabot vu" all over again. I immediately updated my wardrobe, with somewhat messy results. Speaking of messiness and words, Jerry Brewer, in a 2007 *Seattle Times* article (Feb. 4, 2007), wrote of " … words and thoughts that spill from his mouth and splatter everywhere." I agree with George Herbert (1593-1633) who wrote, "Fine words dress ill deeds." Here are some fine words about my dressy jabot and my ill deeds:

jabot

In my **jabot**, I sipped *Bordeaux,* ate *cassoulet* and sweet
gateau –
   And dribbled drips, and dropped *morceaux.*

In frothy lace, I first said grace, then savored spicy
bouillabaisse,
   And dirtied more than just my face.

In flourishes and flirty frills, I'm victim of cascading spills
   From cocktails, canapés, mixed grills.

In my frou-frou, I slurped *ragout,* and left a stain.
Or maybe two.
   Well, let's be honest, quite a few.

Alas, my ruffles now sport truffles, chocolate mousse,
éclairs, cream puffles,
   Crème brulee. Oh, how that stuff'll

Ooze and spurt and squirt and bounce, and turn my striking,
racy flounce
   Into a sight swine would renounce.

I should have eaten ruffle-less, or used a napkin, I confess.
   My fine **jabot** is quite a mess. 2007

ken

François Rabelais (c. 1494-1553) wrote:

> To a man of understanding, only a word is necessary.

With jabot, perhaps the word should have been napkin. Or bib.

Speaking of men of understanding or perception, there's a lot that remains beyond the understanding of most of us. William Alexander (1826-1894), in *Johnny Gibb of Gushetneuk,* wrote of:

> Acts of mind so rapid and minute as to elude the ken of consciousness.

Beyond our ken, in other words.

---

ken, noun (kĕn)
Perception; understanding. Range of vision, insight, or perception. View; sight.
Verb, to know (a person or thing); to recognize.

Here's a little verse from Agnes Kendrick Gray (b. 1894?) in "The Shepherd to the Poet":

> Sure, 'tis God's ways is very quare,
> An' far beyont my ken,
> How o' the selfsame clay he makes
> Poets an' useful men.

I try not to take umbrage. Instead, I add my own musings – my Verse, Re-Verse opposite – keeping in mind the words of Voltaire (1694-1778):

> If God made us in His image, we have certainly returned the compliment.

ken

Just think how strange the ways of men.

  With earthly ends and odds,

Clay, stone, and words, plus mortal **ken**,

  We make convenient gods. 2001

 **lucubration**

Ken. Perception. Understanding. Where do we get it?
One answer is obvious: study. In his "Author's Apology" to
The Pilgrim's Progress, John Bunyan (1628-1688) wrote:

> Things that seem to be hid in words obscure,
> Do but the Godly mind the more allure;
> To study what those sayings should contain
> That speak to us in such a Cloudy strain.

A note of caution, though, from Ben Jonson (c.1573-1637):

> The study of words is the first distemper of learning.

Speaking of study and words, here's an interesting word you might
want to trot out now and then when you're trying to impress
someone with your own level of scholarship:

---

lucubration, noun (loo kyoo **bray'** shŭn)
From the Latin, lucubrare, to work by lamplight; to study at
night.
Laborious, intensive study or meditation.
Also, the writing produced by such study, often expressed in
the plural.
Sometimes used to mean pedantic or pretentious writing.

Immoderate lucubration with overstrained mental exertion.
Feuchtersleben's *Psychical Medicine*

My father loved words and humorous verse, and he was a devoted
Bible scholar. He also used to doze a bit in the evenings, "reading"
in his easy chair.

I wrote this verse for him on his eighty-eighth birthday:

lucubration

How wondrous fine to contemplate

That Oscar A is eighty-eight.

He looks a youthful sixty-nine –

His features firm, nose aquiline –

(Excuse me. Servitude to rhyme

Compels a fib from time to time.)

There's nothing hooked about his schnozz.

It's classic, straight. No, our applause

Is overdue and well deserved,

Because this man's so well preserved.

His gait is spry; his wit acute.

Puns keep forthcoming. And astute,

And clear and lucid, wise and sage

(Unusual for one his age)

Are **lucubrations** of great weight.

Hypotheses he'll postulate,

As studiously, with his book,

He hovers deep in thought. But look –

These reveries (at second peep) –

Are simply Oscar A .... Asleep. 2000

mot juste

It was Anonymous (or Unknown) who wisely and facetiously advised:

> Don't use a big word where a diminutive one will suffice.

Anonymous was right, of course. And droll! It has never been my intention to highlight arcane (recondite, abstruse, esoteric, recherché) words. Even though I found the word lucubration amusing, perhaps I should have let dozing Dads lie.

Why indeed do we need big words when, as Robert Bresson (1901-1999) correctly stated:

> The most ordinary word, when put into place, suddenly acquires brilliance.

Noah Adams wrote:

> The correct word slips into its place in a sentence with a solid "ker-chunk."

And that's the never-ending challenge of writing – hearing that "ker-chunk" – finding that correct word or expression – the

---

mot juste, noun (moh **zhoost'**)
French.
The precise, perfect, exactly correct word or expression.

Ford Madox Ford (1873-1939), speaking of Joseph Conrad, wrote:

> Conrad spent the day finding the mot juste,
> and then killed it.

I'm still looking for the mot juste (and rhyming in the process). I just hope I won't murder it when I do find it:

mot juste

Oh, what would give the struggling, striving scrivener a
boost?

Creative juices flowing freely? Imagery unloosed?
Apt metaphors in multitudes, and adjectives profuse?
And similes and phrases clear, and prose that's unabstruse?
An opus wildly popular, best-selling, mass-produced?
Acclaim and rave reviews and fame and ego *très* seduced?
A place in literary lore? Bold listings in *Who's Who*s?
Appointment as the century's most luminary muse?
The opportunity to rule the literary roost?

Yes, all would please the writer. That's quite easily
deduced!

But what would really satisfy (the author's Golden Goose)

Is finding that elusively, precisely right **mot juste.**   1999

nonage

It's good to be on the lookout for just the right word. However, consider the words of Alfred North Whitehead (1861-1947):

> An enormous part of our mature experience cannot be expressed in words.

In this case, the mot juste is superfluous.

Our mature experience. That's a good introduction to our next word, which actually means just the opposite. Our word embodies youth and immaturity.

Eric Hoffer (1902-1983) wrote:

> One might equate growing up with a mistrust of words.

Here's a word people of all ages can trust:

> **nonage,** noun (**nahn'** ĭj or **nohn'** ĭj)
> The period of youth or minority, during which one is legally underage.
> A lack of maturity.

"… the brook we leaped so nimbly in our nonage." R. S. Hillyer

Immanuel Kant (1724-1804) defined nonage as the "inability to use one's understanding without another's guidance," and defined enlightenment as emergence from this "self-imposed nonage."

Our verse has to do with an old fellow who doesn't share Kant's outlook. He'd like to re-impose his nonage, shed maturity, and revert to a more youthful time. I'm reminded of lines from Bob Dylan's (b. 1941) "My Back Pages":

> I was so much older then,
> I'm younger than that now.

nonage

I'm in my second **nonage**. What I mean

Is simply that I'm younger than I seem.

The graying hair? The slowing gait? A ruse!

I'm just a lad in orthopedic shoes.

In these declining years, these golden days,

I'm going through an awkward, boyish phase.

Impatient with propriety's constraints,

I'm more disposed to sinners than to saints.

I've been a model citizen. Guess what?

It's time for kicking heels, and parting shot!

I've paid my dues. I've played by all the rules;

I'm entering the Hallowed Hall of Fools.

Convention? Bah! My dignity's kaput:

I'm in my second **nonage**, simply put! 2001

oleaginous

I'm not sure quite how we got to the subject of age, old age particularly, since our last word had to do with youth.

However, since we're on the topic, here's another verse about an old man by Ogden Nash (1902-1971):

> There was an old man of Calcutta,
> Who coated his tonsils with butta,
>> Thus converting his snore
>> From a thunderous roar
> To a soft oleaginous mutta.

An Italian proverb states:

> Smooth words do not flay the tongue.

Butter (or should I say butta?) is a smooth word. Here's another:

---

oleaginous, adj. (**oh** lee **ăj'** ŭn ŭs)
Of, concerning, resembling, or like oil; oily.
From the Latin oleaginous, of an olive tree.
Hence, oily in an insincerely polite manner. Offensively ingratiating. Unctuous, greasy, smooth, fawning, slick, obsequious, smarmy, sebaceous.

The Psalmist *Psalms 55:21* wrote of someone with "words … smoother than butter … softer than oil …" Unfortunately, that someone had war in his heart as well. Perhaps he was the type described above – insincere and oily. Oleaginous.

But back to Ogden Nash's old man from Calcutta.
Coating his tonsils?
Can you believe it?
I take exception. Via verse, of course:

oleaginous

Oleaginous coat,
spread on larynx or throat,
gets my vote
    as a treatment extreme.
Can tonsillar greasing
turn nocturnal wheezing
unpleasing
    into a sweet dream?

Yet our whimsical bard
writes of uvular lard.
(Such a card!)
    We're amused, but retort,
with an unctuous mutter,
a smarmy and utter-
ly slick,
    oleaginous snort! 2000

Procrustean

That previous verse from Ogden Nash just happens to be one of my favorite types of humorous verse: the limerick.

As I've been writing this vocabulary verse, I've yielded to temptation several times and used the limerick format.

My next verse is such an example. It's also an example of a dilemma described by my favorite wordsmith, Willard R. Espy (1910-1999):

> There is no conventional way to rhyme some words. However, it is frequently possible to adapt the method of Procrustes – stretching the victims when they are too short or, more often, lopping something off if they are too long.

The method of Procrustes is

Procrustean, adj. (prō **crŭs'** tee ŭn) also **procrustean**
Exhibiting merciless disregard for individual differences or special circumstances. Tending to produce conformity by violent or arbitrary means.
Procrustes was a mythical Greek giant, who stretched or shortened his captives to make them fit his bed(s). Hence, a Procrustean bed is an arbitrary standard to which exact conformity is forced.

Edgar Allan Poe (1809-1849) mentioned the Procrustean bed in "The Purloined Letter":

> A certain set of highly ingenious resources are, with the Prefect, a sort of Procrustean bed, to which he forcibly adapts his designs.

Zoë Akins (1886-1958) was certainly correct when she said, "The Greeks had a word for it." And I have a limerick for it:

Procrustean

A marvelous word is **Procrustean**.

(Upper case, though preferred's, not a must-ean.)

For a mythical giant,

A Greek, and a tyrant,

Procrustes. No ifs, ands, or buts-ean.

Procrustes had methods despotical,

Unusual, cruel, and methodical:

Stretch, de-leg, behead –

'Til they'd fit in his bed –

All his captives. Now who would've thought-ical!

This Greek still lives on in our glossary.

His name says compliance is boss-ary.

A **Procrustean** bed

Means conform, or you're dead!

Submission enforced at all cost-ary. 1999

quotidian

French poet and dramatist Paul Claudel (1868-1955) wrote in "La Muse qui est la Grace":

> The words I use are everyday words, and yet are not the same.

Procrustean would probably not be considered an everyday word.
Nor would our next word.
That's unfortunate, because that's just what it means.

Speaking of everyday or daily things, Johann Wolfgang von Goethe (1749-1832) wrote:

> One ought, every day at least, to hear a little song, read a good poem, see a fine picture and, if possible, speak a few reasonable words.

Every day at least. Had he been writing in English, he might have used the word

---

quotidian, adj. (kwoh **tĭd'** ee ŭn)
Occurring every day or once daily; daily, everyday.
Belonging to each day; day-to-day, workaday, ordinary, routine, commonplace, mundane.
Sometimes still used as a noun, to mean a daily allotment.

When I think of the word daily – or quotidian – I almost immediately think of the word bread. So I've written a verse that's something of a table grace – a grace for the health-conscious and the entitled, and I've called it "Our Quotidian Bread."

I've done this in spite of the admonition of seventeenth century clergyman and scholar John Spencer (1630-1693) that "Common and quotidian thoughts are beneath the grace of a Verse."

quotidian

Our Quotidian Bread

Give us this day our **quotidian** bread.

Please, not the white bread, though. Nine-grain, instead.

Home-baked, from hand-milled flour, ground with a stone;

Complex in carbs, and organically grown;

Bursting with fiber and roughage. Replete

With natural goodness from whole, unbleached wheat.

Give us our bread, Lord, and once we have dined,

May we be fortified. Pure. Unrefined. 2007

rumination

That put me in a somewhat prayerful mood.
There's a very familiar Bible verse that continues this mood and is a good introduction to our next word, as well. *Psalms 19:14*, in the *King James Version*, reads:

> May the words of my mouth, and the meditations of my heart, be acceptable in Thy sight, O Lord, my strength and my Redeemer.

The meditations of my heart.
Here's another good word for meditation:

---

rumination, noun (**roo** mih **nay'** shŭn)
The act of pondering; meditation. Contemplation, reflection, musing, thoughtfulness, introspection, intent consideration.
Also, the act or process of chewing cud.
Verb, ruminate.
From the Latin ruminare, to chew the cud, to turn over in the mind.

Charles Dickens (1812-1870) has the line in *Great Expectations*:

> "There's one thing you may be sure of, Pip," said Joe, after some rumination, "namely, that lies is lies."

In *Othello*, Shakespeare (1564-1616) used the word, too:

> Speak to me as to thy thinkings,
> As thou dost ruminate, and give thy worst of thoughts
> The worst of words.

Here are some of my ruminations on the subject:

rumination

May the words which pass my lips
Be devoid of Freudian slips.
May my musings, as they ought,
Be with virtuousness fraught.
May each utterance and statement
Ring pristine without abatement.
May my thoughts and meditations,
Ponderings, and **ruminations**
All eschew the coarse and earthy;
And my wan attempts at mirth be
Lacking innuendo comic,
Unrefined, or anatomic. 2000

Stygian

We've just heard from the *King James Version*. And we heard from Shakespeare, writing of the worst of thoughts and the worst of words. Shakespeare (1564-1616) also wrote in *The Rape of Lucrece*:

> This helpless smoke of words …

And in *King John* is the line:

> They shoot but calm words folded up in smoke …

Smoke. Keep that in the back of your mind.

Meanwhile, read this description of the worst of customs. It was introduced into England at the turn of the century – that is, the turn from the sixteenth to the seventeenth century.

Here's what none other than King James I of England said about this new fad:

> A custom loathsome to the eye, hateful to the nose, harmful to the brain, dangerous to the lungs, and in the black, stinking fumes thereof, nearest resembling the horrible Stygian smoke of the pit that is bottomless.

Stygian, adj. (**stĭj'** ee ŭn) also stygian
Of or relating to the river Styx, a river in the underworld over which the souls of the dead were ferried.
Hence gloomy, dark, hellish, infernal.

What custom was King James describing?

Perhaps you've heard of the King James aversion?
If not, read on. Come to think of it, read on anyway!

50

Stygian

Have you ever heard of the King James aversion –
　To smoking?　(Offensive to mind, sight, and smell?)
Suffice it to say, no amount of coercion
　Could sway Jim to take up this habit from hell.

Those fumes from a horrible, bottomless pit
　In King James a vision of Hades evoked.
"It's loathsome, black, stinking, and I would submit,"
　He smoldered, "a **Stygian** un-holy smoke!"　1999

T trenchant

King James certainly didn't pull any punches. Forceful and pointed, his words were both blunt and incisive, if that's possible.

Is there anyone who would deny that words can be extremely forceful? Confucius (551-479 BC) wrote:

> Without knowing the force of words, it is impossible to know men.

Add a slightly caustic quality to this forcefulness and incisiveness, and you have the very useful adjective,

---

trenchant, adj. (**trĕnch'** ŭnt)
Penetrating, incisive, caustic, or keen. Also, forceful, effective, sharply or clearly defined, as a trenchant policy or argument.

> The trenchant blade, Toledo trusty,
> For want of fighting was grown rusty.
> Samuel Butler (1612-1680)

Mid-nineteenth century poet Phoebe Cary (1824-1871) used our word in this verse:

> Thou hast battled for the right
> With many a brave and trenchant word
> And shown us how the pen may fight
> A mightier battle than the sword.

Many brave and trenchant words have been directed against smoking, and four hundred years later, the battle continues.

Here's a trenchant verse:

trenchant

James had a penchant for the **trenchant**;
    His logic keen, biting, and sharp.
Jim's proclivity was to brevity;
    Incisive were his remarks.

Jim's mental vigor tended to trigger
    Comments which mirrored his views.
Even Jim's banter was colored with candor,
    So no one was ever confused

About Jim's opinions. Yet even his minions,
    Who touted his vigorous mind,
Admitted his bluntness and forceful up-frontness
    Made friends few and quite hard to find. 1999

ululate

King James used words as effective tools to get his point across.

Or did he? Historian and social philosopher Eugen Rosenstock-Huessy (1888-1973) wrote in *Out of Revolution, Autobiography of Western Man*:

> **Words** are **not** our **tools**; since Adam first called things good and evil, men have cried, spoken, shrieked, screamed, sung, called, and commanded because they **must**, not because they **would**. True language is an expression of necessity, **not a tool** in man's hand. (Highlighting mine.)

I'll continue to believe that words are very effective tools.

However, whether we agree or disagree, we all have at some time felt that we must cry, speak, shriek, scream, sing, call, command – and especially scream and shriek. Here's a good word to keep in mind when you've reached that point:

> **ululate,** verb (**ŭl'** yoo lāt)
> To howl, wail, or lament. To utter howling, shrill sounds.
> To howl, as a dog or a wolf; hoot, as an owl;
> From the Latin ululare –of imitative origin.

In a 1991 episode of *Home Improvement*, Tim's next-door-neighbor, Wilson, tries to explain the concept:

> No Tim. I'm ululating.
> No, no, no, Tim. Ululating is a Middle Eastern custom expressing joy and sorrow.
> Sorrow, because I can't ululate.

Here's a verse for those of us who could use some "Primal Ululating" therapy:

ululate

They're not your fault, of course, these tricks of evil fate.
Your path is strewn with obstacles that aggravate.
Your troubles mount sky-high, and tensions escalate.
Your tolerance is tried to the extreme.

Incompetence, deceit – annoy, exasperate;
Dilemmas multiply and snafus won't abate;
Your pressure valve's about to burst. So – **ululate**.
Just howl it out, and scream the primal scream! 2009

vacillate

Whether the pointed, forceful opinion of King James, or the trenchant delivery of "Jim," or the last-resort ululations of our previous verse, we know where the speaker stands. There's no equivocating, no wavering, no fence-sitting.

There's something to be said for taking a bit of time and thought in making a decision. We all know, however, how frustrating it is to deal with someone who either cannot decide, or who keeps changing positions. Fortunately, there was at least one decision maker among our founding fathers.

Abigail Adams (1744-1818) wrote in a letter to her husband John:

> Shall we not be despised by foreign powers for hesitating so long at a word?

Hesitating. Being indecisive. People with such habits could be said to

---

vacillate, verb (**văs'** uh lāt)
To waver. To fluctuate in opinion or mind; be inconstant. To be indecisive or irresolute. To alternate between different opinions or courses of action.
To oscillate, or sway back and forth, to and fro.

Others have weighed in on the issue, as well. Here are just two:

> O damned vacillating state!
> Alfred, Lord Tennyson, "Supposed Confessions"

> Vacillation is the prominent feature of weakness of character. Voltaire

Consider the devastating, shattering effects of fence-sitting on one well-known fellow:

vacillate

Humpty's on the balustrade;
Humpty's fallen, I'm afraid.
Neither glue, nor magic mastic
Can return this life-sized plastic
Egghead to his heretofore.

Straddling walls? And sitting fences?
What this really represents is
Indecision. That is all.
Vacillating caused this fall.
It's a simple metaphor. 2009

wroth

Shakespeare (1564-1616) – we seem to hear from him a lot! – wrote in *Henry VI, Part III*:

> These were her words, utter'd with mad disdain: …

Vacillating is usually not a part of the picture when angry words are uttered.

A Kashmiri proverb advises that:

> A word stirs up anger or love.

Anger or love. What about anger **and** love? The two can create a volatile combination.

Imagine modifying our vocabulary from angry to the slightly more old-fashioned wroth, and adding love to the equation.

We leave no doubt as to where we stand.

---

wroth, adj. (rŏth)
Angry. Vehemently incensed. Stirred to wrath; moved to ire or indignation; greatly exasperated. Beside oneself, enraged, livid, maddened, infuriated, fuming.
Middle English, from Old English.
Perhaps at one time used as a noun. Consider this line from William Shakespeare (1564-1616), *Merchant of Venice: II, ix*:
Patiently to bear my wroth …

Samuel Taylor Coleridge (1772-1834) wrote the lines in *Christabel*:

> And to be wroth with the one we love
> Doth work like madness in the brain.

He must have had an encounter with the next speaker!

wroth

He's done it again. He's made me see red.

I'm blowing a gasket. I'm hot in the head.

I'm fit to be tied. And – if truth be said –

My sanity's hanging, but just by a thread.

I'm mad as a hornet. My patience is fried.

Hot under the "choler," I'm electrified.

I'm livid. I'm crazed, with intensified

Schemes for revenge. (Justified homicide!)

I'm worked to a frenzy. I'm all in a froth.

I'm wraving. I'm wraging. I'm wrabid. I'm **wroth**! 2006

xanthic

Words have color, too. Learned Hand (1872-1961) wrote, "Words are chameleons, which reflect the colour of their environment."

We've just seen red. Let's take a look at yellow. James J. Kilpatrick (b. 1920) wrote:

> We see words that blow like leaves in the winds of autumn ... golden words, bronze words, words that catch the light like opals.

Well, yellow isn't mentioned specifically. However, Kilpatrick gave us some good synonyms for yellow. Here's another:

---

xanthic, adj. (**zăn'** thĭk)
Yellow. Of, relating to, or tending toward a yellow or yellowish color.
Imparting a yellow color, such as a compound (e.g. xanthic acid) which produces a yellow hue.
Xanthic colors (opposed to cyanic) are those colors of flowers having some tinge of yellow.
Xanthous, by the way, refers more to hair and complexion, e.g. characterized by or having yellowish, red, auburn, or brown hair and a light, fair, or yellow complexion.

An old *Florist's Journal* (1886) writes of one bloom:

> A most uncommon combination of colours – cyanic and xanthic tints in one and the same flower.

Steven Sills writes of another:

> ... ornamental designs engraved on tombstones, xanthic blooms of Magnolia trees, ...

Flowers are all well and good. However, here's a verse about a young woman in a xanthic frock. Perhaps you've heard of her.

xanthic

Cinderella, **xanthic** clad,

Went upstairs to kiss a lad.

By coincidence (I'm told!)

He, too, had on shades of gold.

Ochroid, amber, tawny, cream,

Saffron, flaxen, wheat, citrine,

Aureate, with lemon twist –

How many times was Ella kissed?   2000

yesteryear

Some of you may recall school recesses on the playground, jumping rope. (Remember? Two playmates, usually girls, turning the rope, and the rest lined up waiting a turn, except for the one or two girls actually jumping?) The tradition was to chant jumping rhymes. For example:

> All last night and the night before,
> Twenty-four robbers came to my door ...

In case you missed it, the previous verse, xanthic, was a take-off on a favorite jump-rope rhyme:

> Cinderella, dressed in yella,
> Went upstairs to kiss a fella.
> By mistake she kissed a snake,
> How many doctors did it take?
> (Count the jumps ...)

For me, the above ditties make this quote from South African novelist Peter Abrahams (b. 1919) ring especially true:

> The words dripped on my consciousness, sank into my being, and carried me away to the magic long ago of once upon a time.

Nothing new in this word, just magic, once-upon-a-time

---

yesteryear, noun (**yĕs'** tr yĭr)
Time past; yore. Former times, past time, auld lang syne.

...where are the snows of yesteryear? (ou sont les neiges d'antan?) François Villon (c. 1431-1463) *Ballade des Dames du Temps Jadis.*

Here are some of my reminiscences from yesteryear:

yesteryear

Childhood memories include:
Sunday school, cats, comfort food
(Soup of chicken-noodle ilk,
Snickerdoodles, chocolate milk);
Berry picking, summer bliss.

Practicing the clarinet;
Red formica dinette sets;
Jump ropes, jacks, and lost skate keys;
Slumber parties, spelling bees;
Puppy love, and kitten's kiss.

Loafers, cinch belts, *Our Miss Brooks;*
Ducktails, *Archie* comic books;
Ninety-nine-cent smorgasbords;
Burma-Shaves, and running boards;
Hand-me-downs from bigger sis.

Snapshots from our **yesteryears**:
Hula hoops and Mouseketeers;
Girl Scouts, Peechees, ponytails;
Reader's Digest in the mail.
Memories are made of this. 2002

zabaglione

Had meter and rhyme allowed, I would have included tapioca pudding among the comfort foods of yesteryear.

Instead, I've done the next best thing. I've included a recipe for something even sweeter. It makes for a sweet ending to this half of our book.

Robert Browning (1812-1889) wrote:

> For what are the voices of birds
> Ay, and of beasts – but words, our words,
> Only so much more sweet?

Words, sweeter even than tapioca pudding or

---

zabaglione, noun (zah bahl **yoh'** nay)
An Italian custard – a mixture of egg yolks, sugar, and wine (usually Marsala) or fruit juice, beaten over simmering water until thickened and creamy. It is often served immediately over fruit; although it can be chilled to be eaten later.
The French term is sabayon.

One minute the penultimate course of a splendid meal sat before me: mixed berries zabaglione, an artful confection of glazed fruit and delicate pastry horns reclining in a puddle of seductive white sauce.
Capital Style, October, 1998.

For me, the penultimate cookbook would be written in verse. Here's a recipe for the dessert section that will enable you to play in puddles – of seductive white sauce:

zabaglione

Zabaglione. Oh, how sweet.

Fun to say, to make, to eat.

> Take eight egg yolks. Beat them up.
> Add some sugar. (One-half cup.)
> Add Marsala, or sweet wine –
> One-half cup will be just fine.
> Next, get out your boiler (double).
> Bring some water to a bubble.
> Over this your mixture goes.
> Keep on beating, I propose,
> 'Til a thickened frothy cream,
> Custard-like – dessert supreme.
> Serve it right away on fruit.
> Now, enjoy. That's all there's tuit.

Zabaglione. Oh, how sweet.

Fun to say, to make, to eat. 2000

zephyr

Z – a sweet ending, the ultimate zabaglione dessert.
Now, let's put the alphabet in reverse and go back to A.

If you're treating this book as a weekly almanac, you're into July right now.

What are we looking for in July? Lord Byron (1788-1824) wrote in *Don Juan*:

> 'Tis something, nothing, words, illusion, wind.

Wind. A little breeze would be delightful.
Here's the perfect word for a hot July day:

---

zephyr, noun (**zĕf'** r)
A gentle breeze. The west wind, literally, and when used as such, may be capitalized.
Can also mean something that is airy, passing, or insubstantial.
A soft, gauzy, light fabric or garment.
From the Greek Zephyros "the west wind" (sometimes personified as a god).

I wonder if Lord Byron was feeling a mild, refreshing breeze when he wrote the above words! Likewise Thomas Gray (1716-1771), when he wrote in "The Bard":

> Fair laughs the morn and soft the zephyr blows,
> While proudly riding o'er the azure realm.

Zephyr. What a pleasant word. It even sounds refreshing.
No need to get carried away with it, though, like the "sort" described in the next verse.

66

zephyr

You know the sort, I would purport –
  intent on sounding clever.
They sneer at words like wind and air,
  and call a breeze a **zephyr**.

They love cat's paws, and shout hurrahs
  at soughs and sounds aeolian.
Can't get enough of gentle puffs;
  and whiffles they're extol-ian.

It's *declassé*, they think, to say,
  "It's breezy out." No. Never.
They're daft for wafts and die for drafts, and say,
  "How 'bout that **zephyr**!"

When these folks chat or chew the fat,
  it's always their endeavor
To *tête-a-tête*. Or better yet,
  they strive to shoot the **zephyr**.

Auf Wiederseh'n to wind-swept manes.
  Since erudition blesses
Our cultured bunch, I've got a hunch
  they've **zephyr** in their tresses!

In the event they've "up and went,"
  Gone bye-bye. Split. Whatever.
Just rest assured, their phrase preferred
  would be "Gone with the **Zephyr**." 2000

67

yare

When I think of zephyrs, I also think of water. Like Thomas Gray, I picture myself on "the azure realm." Ralph Waldo Emerson (1803-1882) sets the scene for our next word:

> Every day brings a ship,
> Every ship brings a word;
> Well for those who have no fear,
> Looking seaward well assured
> That the word the vessel brings
> Is the word they wish to hear.

This word (the word we "wish to hear," perhaps?) borders on the archaic. I'm going to ignore the words of Julius Caesar (100-44 BC) who advised, "An unusual word should be shunned as a ship would shun a reef." This unusual word relates to ships but can also describe people:

---

yare, noun (yair – rhymes with hair; or yahr, archaic)
Agile, quick, lively.
Nautical – of a ship or vessel – Easy to handle, and responsive to the helm. Maneuverable and responsive.
Archaic – Ready, prepared.

Sir Walter Raleigh (c. 1552-1618) wrote, "The lesser [ship] will come and go, leave or take, and is yare; whereas the greater is slow."

Here's a description from *Mary Queen of Scotland And The Isles*:

> The vessels were yare and scrubbed, and the flagship was draped with garlands of flowers, ropes … that looped around the rails and over the figurehead on the prow. …

Is the next verse about a vessel? A person? You decide.

yare

I'm in agile repair. Yes, I'm fit,
Showing, no wear or tear – not a bit.

Garlands give me an air

Lively, quick, debonair.

I've got vigor to spare,

Not a worry or care.

Life's a shipshape affair,

And I'm loaded for bear.

See how extr'ordinaire my bowsprit?

I'm so – what's the word? – **Yare.** Yes, that's it! 2010

Xanadu

We've experienced soft breezes and a glimpse of the ocean. And vessels.

Add a beautiful sky, and what could be more idyllic?
Walt Whitman's (1819-1892) line in "Reconciliation" comes to mind:

> Word over all, beautiful as the sky, ...

This next word conjures up the most beautiful of places, a place described in a very famous poem by Samuel Taylor Coleridge (1772-1834):

> In Xanadu did Kubla Khan
> A stately pleasure-dome decree: ...

Xanadu, noun (**zăn'** uh doo, or dyoo)
(From Samuel Taylor Coleridge's 1816 poem "Kubla Khan")
A beautiful, idyllic place of great contentment and luxury.
Also, a place suggestive of the Xanadu in Coleridge's poem, the name he gave Kubla Khan's beautiful summer palace, Shang-tu, with its dream-like magnificence and opulence.
Now used to describe any idyllic place, real or imagined.

Here's a slight update to Coleridge from the 1975 TV movie *Sweet Hostage*:

> In Xanadu did I,
> a stately pleasure dome decree.
> And there, from force of habit, I
> only dine with royalty.

Just in case you'd like to find the place – know where to look and what to look for – here's my offering on the topic:

Xanadu

Xanadu,

What are you?

    Stately, splendid, sunny Shangri-la.

    Pleasure dome. Enchanted, mystic spa.

    Beulah. Bliss. A place of mystic worth.

    Paradise. Elysium on earth.

Xanadu,

Where are you?

    Look for walls and towers girdling round.

    Gardens bright. Rills. Fountains. Cedarn ground.

    Deep romantic chasms in a dream.

    East of Eden. Down a sacred stream.   2002

wanton

Are you still in Xanadu? In Shangri-la?
Are you still feeling a gentle breeze? A zephyr?

Our next word can also be used to describe a breeze. Shakespeare
(1564-1616) used it this way in his poem "The Blossom":

> On a day – alack the day! –
> Love, whose month is ever May,
> Spied a blossom passing fair
> Playing in the wanton air:

" … the wanton air." Playful. Undisciplined.
But wanton has other definitions, too:

---

wanton, adj. (**wahnt'** n)
  1. Frolicsome, playful, spoiled, hard to control,
     undisciplined, even unruly, e.g. "the wanton air."
  2. Lewd, bawdy; causing sexual excitement; lustful,
     sensual.
  3. Senselessly cruel; unprovoked in meanness or
     gratuitous maliciousness; deliberately unjust.
From Middle English wan and towen, lacking in discipline.

They that dally nicely with words may quickly make them wanton.
William Shakespeare (1564-1616)

I dallied with words a bit – nicely I hope you'll agree – and made
them into a "wanton" verse:

wanton

Oh, the **wanton** air ...
      is an atmosphere ...
That's playful, prankish, or unruly.
It's a frisky breeze ...
      wafting through the trees,
But could do mischief, too. Unduly!

Now, a **wanton** dame's ...
      not at all the same ...
She's lustful, sensual, lubricious;
Unrestrained and lewd ...
      with an attitude ...
That's loose, risqué, and injudicious.

Then, the **wanton** act ...
      (unprovoked, in fact ...)
The hardest wantonness to take:
Undeserved and mean ...
      cruel and unforeseen;
Maliciousness for its own sake.   2000

vapidity

We touched on a certain kind of woman in the last verse: the wanton woman.

Our next verse targets another type of woman, a "dumb" one.

G. C. Lichtenberg (1742-1799) wrote in *Aphorisms*:

> We have no words for speaking of wisdom to the stupid.
> He who understands the wise is wise already.

In our case, we don't speak **to** – so much as **of** – our certain kind of woman. She's the frequent butt of jokes and innuendo: the dumb blond.

I have to confess that, a blond myself, I laugh along with everyone else at "blond jokes." August Brown asks in a *Florida Times-Union* article (Jun 30, 2003. p. C.1) why there are

> ... cultural stigmas (superficiality, intellectual vapidity) associated with being blond.

---

vapidity, noun (vă **pĭd'** ĭ tee)
The quality or state of being vapid.
Staleness, dullness, insipidity, flatness, jejuneness, tastelessness – often used in reference to persons, places, entertainments, discourse, and intellectualism (or lack!) in general.

> ... the truth is that fullness of soul can sometimes overflow in utter vapidity of language, for none of us can ever express the exact human measure of his needs or his thoughts or his sorrows; ...
> Gustave Flaubert (1821-1880), *Madame Bovary*

Here's a test for vapidity (if you're not already a blond):

vapidity – To brunettes (and darker):

Do blonds have more **vapidity**?
Does this myth have validity?
With relative rapidity,
   Find out. Undo that bun.

> *Mix color potion ("Golden Dream")*
> *With pure, enriching, toning cream.*
> *Apply to hair and spread all through.*
> *Wait twenty minutes, then shampoo.*

You're blond! How's your lucidity?
Has it, with great fluidity,
Transmuted to stupidity?
   And … are you having fun? 2003

umbrageous

We've covered red (wroth), yellow (xanthic), and shades of hair color. Words themselves can have shades, too. Mark Twain (1835-1910) wrote:

> Have you no sense of shades of meanings in words?

In this next word and verse, however, we're dealing simply with shade itself. Once again, if you're using this book as a weekly almanac, you probably find yourself looking for shady spots.

Here's another word for shady:

---

umbrageous adj. (ŭm **bray**' jŭs)
Shady. Abounding in shade. Providing or creating shade.
From the Latin umbra, shade. (Think umbrella.)
Can also mean prone to take offense. (Think umbrage.)

Henry James (1843-1916) wrote:

> Summer afternoon – summer afternoon; to me those have always been the two most beautiful words in the English language.

He must have had access to air conditioning. Or zephyrs.
Or wanton air. For those who don't, here's some advice from Frederic William Farrar (1831-1903), in his novel *Darkness and Dawn*:

> Everyone should wander at will about the green copses, and the umbrageous retreats.

That advice was the inspiration for the following verse:

umbrageous

What is so rare in July, or in August?

When sultriness reigns? When temperatures dog us?

At high noon, especially, what can't be beat

For dodging the heat?   An **umbrageous** retreat!

Dash air conditioning. Folks, here's the ticket:

Wander at will in a green copse, or thicket,

Or forest primeval, or arbor, or glade –

Whatever. The answer's a spot in the shade. 2009

T tuffet

While you're wandering about an umbrageous retreat, perhaps you'll encounter that friend from your childhood, Little Miss Muffet.

Did you ever wonder just where you might find a tuffet? Would it be a comfortable roost? Certainly, comfort cannot be overlooked. Alfred, Lord Tennyson (1809-1892) wrote:

> My lighter moods are like to these,
> That out of words a comfort win.

And, what about those curds and whey?
Following are two views of Miss Muffet and her tuffet adventure.

---

tuffet, noun (**tŭf'** ĭt)
(A derivation of tuft.)
A clump or tuft of grass. A low seat, such as a stool.
From the Old French *touffel* – a little tuft.
In existence since the mid-sixteenth century and given new life by the nineteenth century nursery rhyme:
Little Miss Muffet sat on a tuffet, Eating her curds and whey.

Here's one verse:

> Little Miss Muffet discovered a tuffet,
> (Which never occurred to the rest of us)
> And, as 'twas a June day, and just about noonday,
> She wanted to eat – like the rest of us:
> Her diet was whey, and I hasten to say
> It is wholesome and people grow fat on it.
> The spot being lonely, the lady not only
> Discovered the tuffet, but sat on it.
> Guy Wetmore Carryl (1873-1904)

Here's my Re-Verse:

78

tuffet

"So . . . this is a **tuffet**?" cried Little Miss Muffet.

"I think I'd prefer a divan,

Soft sofa, or settee, 'cuz (lest I seem testy)

This tuffet's too hard on my can."

"And this gross *déjeuner*. Curds and whey? What are they?

They're loathsome, disgusting, repug-

nant. Regrettable seating. Inedible eating;

And now, this arachnid-like bug!" 2000

susurrus

Let's stay in the woods just a bit longer.
Dusk is approaching. Listen.
Can you hear the sounds Lord Byron (1788-1824) described
in *Parisina*?

> It is the hour when from the boughs
> The nightingale's high note is heard;
> It is the hour when lovers' vows
> Seem sweet in every whisper'd word;
> And gentle winds and waters near,
> Make music to the lonely ear.

Or the sounds described by Mary Hunter Austin (1868-1934) in her
poem "Whisper of the Wind":

> Whisper of the wind along the sage,
> Only wait till I can get the word –
> Never was it printed in a page,
> Never was it spoken, never heard.

The boughs, waters, gentle winds, sage. The words. Whispered.
Here's a wonderful, evocative word to use for whisper:

---

susurrus, noun (soo **sur'** ŭs)
A whisper. A soft rustling or murmuring sound.
From the Latin, to whisper.
Of imitative (onomatopoeic) origin.

> The chant of their vespers,
> Mingling its notes with the soft susurrus and sighs of the branches.
> Henry Wadsworth Longfellow (1807-1882)

Susurrus. What a lovely word. I did a (very) quick search in poetry
collections for poets' descriptions of whispering things. Here is the
resulting verse:

susurrus

Sighs from the wistful, and wind in the boughs;
Kind words, and curses, and shyly-voiced vows;
Pine branches, lovers, and gaggles of girls;
Secretive liars, and dry leaves in whirls;
Ocean waves lapping, and taffeta gowns –
Rustling, or rippling, or whispering sounds.
Poets and dreamers and sages assure us,
Such are the murmuring tones of **susurrus**. 2009

rodomontade

If the whispering, murmuring sounds of susurrus are pleasing to you, you may not like the next word.

I'm reminded of a line from Rudyard Kipling (1865-1936):

> For frantic boast and foolish word
> Thy mercy on Thy people, Lord!

Henry Wadsworth Longfellow (1807-1882), in *The Song of Hiawatha*, offers the following:

> Deeds are better things than words are,
> Actions mightier than boastings.

As you might have guessed, it's the boastful word that we're turning to, and it's usually not delivered in soft, whispered tones.

---

rodomontade, noun (rŏd-uh-mŏn-**tayd'** or -**tahd'**)
Pretentious, boastful speech. Inflated language. Boasting, bragging, bluster, gasconade, fanfaronade.
Can also be used as an adjective (boastful or bragging) or a verb (to boast or brag).
French, from Italian rodomontade. From Rodomonte, a great but arrogant Saracen leader in Italian epics of the late fifteenth and early sixteenth centuries.
I prefer the second pronunciation, (tahd on the final syllable). Since most dictionaries prefer the long ā, I've compromised.

Nicholas Barber, "In the Very Bleak Midwinter," *Independent,* January 7, 1996, uses the line:

> . . . the me-me-me rodomontade of macho rap.

Me-me-me. What a novel way to begin a verse:

rodomontade

Me-me-me. Words strut by. A bravado brigade
swaggers past in a blustery ego parade.
Braggadocio, bumptious and brazenly brayed,
in arrogant rhythm. A **rodomontade**.

Me-me-me. There's a stream of words running roughshod,
with boasts much inflated. They puff and they plod,
Pretentious and empty, their beat oompah-pah'd
in arrogant rhythm. A **rodomontade**. 2005

querulous

Whispered words and boastful words. We've heard both. Now, how about a couple of weepy words?

Scottish dramatist and poet, David Mallet (c. 1705-1765) wrote of:

> Words that weep, and strains that agonise.

Here's a word that weeps. (Or whines, anyway.)

---

querulous, adj. (**kwair'** uh lŭs – also **kwair'** yuh lŭs)
Given to complaining; habitually peevish, fretful, or complaining; grumbling. Whining, disagreeable, cranky.

The word is used a lot and is good to keep in mind when you're describing that habitual complainer.

T. S. Eliot (1888-1965) advised:

> Criticism should not be querulous and wasting, all knife and root-puller, but guiding instructive, inspiring.

John Locke (1632-1704) wrote (of children):

> Their crying is of two sorts; either stubborn and domineering, or querulous and whining.

Horace also has this description:

> … testy, querulous and given to praising the way things were when he was a boy.

Locke and Horace both might have been talking about the couple described in our next verse – our "querulous pair-ulous":

querulous

She whimpers, grumbles, gripes, and whines –
Complains. She's always in a fuss.
Her peevish, fretful voice shows signs
Of petulance. It's **querulous**.

He's cranky, disagreeable;
He's gloomy, grouchy, grumpy Gus.
His woes are guarantee-able.
His middle name? It's **Querulous**.

This duo dour – this tearful two –
These advocates of agony –
This plaintive pair – they met. Sparks flew.
Yes, misery loves company! 2000

pule

While we're on the topic of weeping, here's a line from William Shakespeare's (1564-1616) *Two Gentlemen of Verona*:

> I weep myself to think upon thy words.

Our next word is something that might be a pattern of behavior for our querulous pair-ulous.

How many times as children were we admonished for whining?

Had our parents been as concerned with our vocabulary as with our behavior, they might have alternated the suggestion that we stop puling.

> **pule,** verb (pyool)
> To whine, to whimper.
> To speak in a whining or querulous tone.

> And then to have a wretched puling fool,
> A whining mammet, ...
> William Shakespeare (1564-1616), *Romeo and Juliet*.

American psychologist and philosopher William James (1842-1910) chastised us:

> What can be more base and unworthy than the pining, puling, mumping mood, no matter by what outward ills it may have been engendered?

For some strange reason, I love the word pule. Just saying it amuses me. Should I ever find myself in a "pining, puling, mumping mood," I'll simply remember the following verse:

pule

No one loves me, I'm sure, and my mood's in decline;
I need TLC. Think I'll whine.

Unnoticed. Unpampered. This world's so uncivil;
I feel so forlorn. Think I'll snivel.

Self-esteem is deflating. My ego's grown limper;
I'm hurt to the quick. Think I'll whimper.

Attention's not coming my way. Life is cruel;
I'm feeling ignored. Think I'll **pule.** 2007

orotund

When we think of whining, puling, querulous speech, we would probably not imagine the following description from the (British) 1840 *Penny Cyclopaedia*:

> ... that natural or improved manner of uttering the elements, which exhibits them with a fulness, (sic) clearness, strength, smoothness, and a ringing or musical quality rarely heard in ordinary speech.

Nor would we imagine this from Mark Twain (1835-1910):

> He liked words, fine words, grand words, rumbling thundering, reverberating words.

What they're talking about is speech that is

---

orotund, adj. (**ohr'** uh tŭnd)
Of a voice: Sonorous, rich. Fuller, stronger, or clearer than for ordinary speaking.
Of a style of speaking: Pompous, grandiloquent. Often used contemptuously to describe inflated speech.
From the Latin term ore rotundo, literally meaning with round mouth.

> Mr. Chutney would have pulled a face as long as a well-known stringed instrument, and ejaculated, in orotund voice, "Alas!"
> Martin Legrand (1843-1882), *Memoirs of a College Freshman*

This is a wonderful word to describe a sonority or style of speech that is so captivating that ideas become secondary in importance, as in our following verse, and as in this quote from John Wilson's (1785-1854) *Noctes Ambrosianae*:

> Would you repeat that again sir, for it soun's sae sonorous that the words droon the ideas?

orotund

So sonorous and powerful he sounds.

His lofty speech my timid heart confounds.

Narration so inflated, **orotund**,

He's got me spellbound, stupefied, and stunned!

That voice profound – how deep and resonant;

His oratory – how grandiloquent.

Those honeyed tones, a deep and mellow blur;

His words – heroic, flowery ... obscure,

Ornately phrased, as verbally he preens.

(And I can barely fathom what he means!)   2009

nimiety

Many speakers, gifted with a sonorous voice, develop an orotund style of speech (as described in our last verse). They often fall in love with the sounds of their own voices. The resulting oral diarrhea gives credence to (again!) Shakespeare's (1564-1616) words, this time from *King Richard II*:

> Where words are scarce, they are seldom spent in vain, ...

Here's a quotation from Louise Erdrich (b. 1954) that follows this train of thought:

> It was just enough to sit there without words.

Scarce words. Without words.

It's true. Often less is more! This next word-verse, however, has to do with more, not less. With excess, even. It's a great word to use occasionally to spice up your speech or writing:

---

nimiety, noun (nih **mī'** uh tee)
More than enough; more than a lot; the state of being too much.
Excess, redundancy, overabundance, plethora, surfeit, superfluity, glut, overkill.
From the Latin nimietas (much; too much), and nimis (excessively).

Get the idea? If not, here's more:

> Mark Broatch examines the glut – or plethora, prog, peck, repletion, supererogation, nimiety – of books on language. "The Gateway to Pedants' Paradise," *Sunday Star-Times*, April 24, 2005.

Here's a verse for those of us for whom "plenty" of nothing is just not enough:

nimiety

Plenty of nothing is what I've got;

Plenty, meaning quite a lot.

Always unsated, though, I want more –

More of nothing. Let it pour,

A lavish profusion of nullity;

Naught? There's not enough for me!

Give me nothing – to excess.

A **nimiety** of nothingness. 2009

mesomorph

Speaking of surfeit, overkill, nimiety and the like, here's a word and a verse about a guy with perhaps a bit too much.

Martha Graham (1894-1991) stated in a March 1985 interview, "The body says what words cannot."

Of course, she was talking of interpretive dance. But consider the following picture, drawn by W. H. Auden (1907-1973), where the body **is** trying to say something:

> Behold the manly mesomorph
> Showing his bulging biceps off, ...

---

mesomorph,   noun   (**mĕz'** uh mōrf' – **mĕs-**)
A mesomorphic person (anatomy).
That is to say, a person characterized by a muscular body.
Powerfully built, athletic, and active. One of the three body-personality types, the other two being:
endomorph (fat, fleshy, sociable, and fond of comfort); and
ectomorph (thin, hard, cerebral, quiet, and reflective).
A "new" word, coined in 1940 by W. H. Shelton.
From meso, plus the Greek morphe (form).

By the way, I should probably note that women can be mesomorphs, too. It's just a body type. Mary Gold, in the *Daily Mail* (London), wrote (March 23, 2010 p.53):

> Before I got married, I saw a dietician who said I was a "mesomorph." That may sound like an alien from Dr. Who, but it actually means I'm not a fatty or a skinny but of an athletic build.

I think that Auden's picture of a mesomorph is the one we are more apt to conjure up, though, and it inspired this verse:

mesomorph

When Muscle Man meets pretty lass,
Behold what strange things come to pass:

He sees her, and his muscles flex.
His chest expands. His abs and pecs
Grow ripples. Mighty biceps taut –
From dead lifts, sit-ups, push-ups, squats –
He postures thus: sucks in his gut;
And bulges thighs and calves and butt.
His every sinew, firm and tight,
Entreats her to admire his might;
Beseeches her to see his brawn,
And be impressed. ... But ... she's long gone.

Heart weighted down he broods, alas,
When **mesomorph** meets pretty lass. 2004

 **lissome**

We seem to have "morphed" to bodies and exercise. Our next word describes another type of body, this one usually associated with females. But first, consider some very active words in general from "verbivore" Richard Lederer (b.1938) in *The Miracle of Language*:

> English is a veritable playground of words – words clambering over jungle gyms, words bouncing up and down on seesaws, words swinging on rings and ringing on swings, words whizzing down sliding boards, words merrily whirling around on merry-go-rounds.

Words – agile, bending, limber, lithe, and

---

lissome, adj. (**lĭs' ŭm**)   Also, **lissom** (esp. British)
From an alteration of lithesome.
Bending easily. Lithe. Gracefully agile. Supple, nimble, pliant, limber, flexible, light-footed, sprightly.

> Her castanets click out in conscious pride;
> Curved throat, arched foot, and lissome-swaying hips, ...
> "The Dancer" by Ednah Proctor (Clarke) Hayes
> (c.1866-1956)

Things other than bodies can be lissome, too:

> The tongues grow lissom under the influence of good fellowship and potent liquor.
> Thomas Alexander Browne (Rolf Boldrewood) (1826-1915)

When I hear the word lissome, I think of ballerinas, and I imagine the following:

lissome

Those limber young things in the corps de ballet:
They leap, and they bound in a graceful *jété*;
They soar through the air with the greatest of ease;
Then, **lissome** and lovely, they sink to their knees.

All postured and elegant in a *plié*,
They gracefully rise, in a slow *relevé*.
Together, a formal and poised menuette,
Then, **lissome** and agile, they all pirouette.

En pointe now, so nimble, they whirl, twirl, and writhe,
Then sweep and glissade, mannered, supple, and lithe.
They capture our hearts, this demure entourage,
Then, **lissome** and winsome, accept our homage. 2000

kith

Words dancing, words exercising, words playing.
How about words just "getting along," or making alliances even?
O. Henry (1862-1910), in his short story "Calloway's Code" in
Whirligigs, wrote:

> Most wonderful of all are words, and how they make
> friends one with another, being oft associated, …

Some words make such good friends with each other that they
seem to be pairs – always together. For example, do you ever see
kith without kin?

> One would be in less danger
> From the wiles of the stranger
> If one's own kin and kith
> Were more fun to be with.
> Ogden Nash (1902-1971)

---

kith, noun (kĭth – rhymes with "with.")
Familiar friends, neighbors, or relatives. Many American
dictionaries list only **kith and kin** –
One's acquaintances and relatives. One's relatives.
From an Old English word meaning country. The alliterative
phrase kith and kin dates from the fourteenth century and
originally meant "country and kinsmen."

> She kissed the lips of kith and kin,
> She laid her hand in mine:
> What more could ask the bashful boy
> Who fed her father's kine?
> John Greenleaf Whittier (1807-1892), "My Playmate"

Here are some pairs of things that go together, all fit into a verse:

Kith is meaningless apart.
It needs a crony. Counterpart.
A bosom buddy. Soulmate. Twin.
It needs its alter ego, kin,
To hobnob with through thick and thin.
Good times or bad, or lose or win.
In love or war. Betwixt, between,
Not one without the other seen.
Through time and tide, they're side by side;
They go as pals, whate'er betide.
Together, they're a partnership.
Like yin and yang, or chips and dip.
Like Tweedledum and Tweedledee,
Their indivisibility
Resembles tonic paired with gin.
One big, happy **kith** and kin.
Sum and substance, French with poodle;
Ebb and flow, kit and kaboodle;
Rock and roll, and horse and buggy;
Hide and seek, and kissy-huggy;
Nip and tuck, and sugar and spice;
Spic-and-span, and naughty and nice;
Bread and butter, fish and chips –
Such mutual relationships
Are symbiotic through and through.
Sidekicks – allies tried and true.
Friends and family. Kin and **kith**.
One must have the other with.
Two little words, yet plain to see,
They're stronger as a family.
Kith and kin, for what it's worth,
You're salt and pepper of the earth! 1999

97

 **jeremiad**

That's quite a collection of words that "get along." Our next verse is about someone who is not getting along very well. Everything seems to be going wrong, and our victim apparently doesn't share the sentiments of Alfred, Lord Tennyson (1809-1892):

> I sometimes hold it half a sin
> To put in words the grief I feel.

Instead, she gives us quite a list of grievances and echoes the feelings of Sir Arthur Helps (1813-1875):

> I could sit down, and mourn, and utter doleful Jeremiads without end.

---

jeremiad, noun (jair' ŭ **mī'** ŭd) Sometimes **Jeremiad** (capitalized), esp. British English.
A long, mournful complaint about one's life or situation. A prolonged lamentation or tale of woe intended to produce compassion, so called from the *Lamentations of Jeremiah* in the *Old Testament*.
Also, a cautionary or angry harangue. A writing or speech expressing grief, distress, lament, or prophecy of doom.
Synonyms: lamentation, lament, complaint, tale of woe, threnody, cri du coeur, ululation.

> A lamentation and an ancient tale of wrong,
> Like a tale of little meaning, tho' the words are strong.
> "The Lotos-Eaters," Alfred, Lord Tennyson (1809-1892)

Here's a modern-day jeremiad – a lamentation and a tale of "little meaning." (Tho' the words are strong.)

jeremiad

Oh, the tales I could tell. Things aren't going so well.
I'm compelled to unload. To confiad.
I've been down with the flu; and I'm feeling so blue.
Entre nous, will my troubles subsiad?
Both the kids have been grounded; my car was impounded,
My faithful hound dog up and diad.
My dress? The cat clawed it. The tax return audit ...
Looookin' bad ... and my patience is triad.
Our poor old roof leaks. The screen door? It squeaks.
I'm trying to take life in striad.
The neighborhood's shot; the porch has dry rot;
The backyard is one big mud sliad.
Our front door was egged; the painter reneged;
And things aren't much better insiad.
The kitchen sink's plugged, and the toilet. I'm bugged,
'Cuz the plumber's too busy. Besiad,
The furnace just quit. The sitter left. Split.
No wonder I'm fit to be tiad.
The front room is trashed. My hard drive just crashed;
Our TV reception's cockiad.
The stove's on the fritz, and cooking's the pits,
I'm at my wit's end. My brain's friad.
The mister's laid off; I can't shake this cough,
In spite of the cure-alls I've triad.
I'm sorry to whine, but my health's in decline;
I'm flabby, tired, sore, bleary-iad.
Things are going to heck; and I get no respeck;
Hence my tale of woe. My **jeremiad**. 1999

I insouciance

Not exactly a lighthearted verse.
Maybe we're due a more buoyant, carefree word.
Dorothy (Lady Temple) Osborne (1627-1695) wrote:

> All letter, methinks, should be as free and easy as one's
> discourse, not studied as an oration, nor made up of hard
> words like a charm.

Free and easy. That quality very well describes our next word:

---

insouciance, noun (ĭn **soo'** see ŭns or in soo **syahns'**)
Lightheartedness, nonchalance; the state of being carefree,
easygoing, happy-go-lucky, buoyant, untroubled, whimsical,
capricious.
insouciant, adj.
Marked by blithe unconcern; nonchalant.

Sir Walter Scott (1771–1832) gives us some synonyms in the
following two selections:

> He was hard-favoured, and, which was worse, his face bore
> nothing of the insouciance, the careless frolicsome jollity
> and vacant curiosity of a sailor on shore.

> This insouciant, light-tempered, and thoughtless
> disposition, conducted Rene … to a hale and mirthful old
> age.

Insouciance – and its adjective counterpart insouciant – are
wonderful words to enliven one's vocabulary. Here are a few more
descriptive terms:

insouciance

Nothing's a nuisance
For those with **insouciance**.
(Lightheartedness. Blithe nonchalance.)

Bad luck never daunts
Those bright **insouciants**.
Their lives are just *par excellence.*

They're breezy, go-easy,
Untroubled, carefree-sy
And happy-go-lucky, to boot.

They're buoyant, *sans souci,*
Almost loosey-goosey;
Capricious, and don't give a hoot. 1999

hunky-dory

For those "bright insouciants" with insouciance, life is more than just par excellence. Life is downright hunky-dory.

English novelist and poet George Meredith (1828-1909) wrote of:

... learned dictionary words giving a hand to street slang.

Our learned dictionary word insouciance has given way to – if not street slang – a very casual word, probably used more in conversation than formal writing or speech.

---

hunky-dory, adj. (**hŭnk'** ee **dohr'** ee)
Quite satisfactory. Fine.
According to *The Barnhart Concise Dictionary of Etymology*, this expression dates from 1866, and perhaps comes from the earlier hunk, in a safe position, all right. Hunk was borrowed from the Dutch honk, goal or home, and further dates back to Middle Dutch, and Frisian, honc, a place of refuge or hiding place.

Sinclair Lewis (1885-1951) used the word in *Babbitt*:

George, old scout, you were sore-headed about something, here a while back. I don't know why, and it's none of my business. But you seem to be feeling all hunky-dory again, ...

So, we're all hunky-dory? We're all copacetic?
From the 2008 movie *Fanboys*

Here's a hunky-dory, copacetic verse:

hunky-dory

Splendid. Super. Smashing. Swell.

(Meaning, things are going well.)

Nifty. Fine-and-dandy. Neat.

(Meaning, things just can't be beat.)

Copacetic. Okay. Cool.

(Meaning, ducky is the rule.)

Tippy-top and peachy-keen.

(Okey-dokey's what we mean.)

Boss. Bodacious. Not half bad.

(Far out. First-rate, may we add.)

Groovy. Great. Good. Gosh-a-glory –

(What we mean is **hunky-dory**.) 2000

gallimaufry

Unlike hunky-dory, but considerably more than insouciance, our next word is a "learned dictionary word." The *Oxford English Dictionary* would undoubtedly be voted the most "learned" of our dictionaries. In *The Meaning of Everything: The Story of the Oxford English Dictionary*, Simon Winchester writes, the *OED* is:

> ... the catalogue of a truly vast emporium of words ...
> ... a perpetual gallimaufry of delights.

A gallimaufry of delights.

A word with edible origins, perhaps this word will satisfy the most "depraved appetite," described by co-authors (most famously of *Mutiny on the Bounty*) James Norman Hall (1887-1951) and Charles Nordhoff (1887-1949), in *Faery Lands of the South Seas:*

> Words, words! In my mind's eye I saw magnificent forests being destroyed, to feed this depraved appetite for words.

---

gallimaufry, noun (găl uh **mah'** free)
A jumble, hodge-podge, stew, medley, hash.
In medieval times, a meat stew, using a cooked leg of mutton, or a chicken perhaps, chopped finely with onions, verjuice (a very acidic juice, common in medieval times, made by pressing unripe grapes), butter and seasonings.
The origin is speculated upon, but essentially unknown.

The ear trieth words, as the mouth tasteth meat. *Job 24:3*

> Were you thinking that those were the words, those
> delicious sounds out of your friends' mouths?
> No, the real words are more delicious than they.
> Walt Whitman (1819-1892), "A Song of the Rolling Earth"

Here is a gallimaufry of some delicious words:

gallimaufry

Words, words, words. A medley, cooked in a
delicious stew;
A cacophony of clauses, concocted *á ragout*;
Adjectives assorted, in an appetizing hash;
A *mélange* of meanings in an aromatic mash.

Words to taste and savor. A variety of verbs,
Nuanced with nouns galore, with complement of herbs.
Words to gulp voraciously. For noshes, nibbles, bites.
Words delectable. A **gallimaufry** of delights. 2009

furbelow

Jonathan Swift wrote in *Gulliver's Travels*:

> Their style is clear, masculine, and smooth, but not florid;
> for they avoid nothing more than multiplying unnecessary
> words, or using various expressions.

We've had words for (essentially) masculine and feminine bodies
(mesomorph and lissome).

Also, going up the alphabet we touched on style with jabot. Like
the "unnecessary words" Swift mentions, the jabot could be
considered a fashion non-necessity. So too, this next word. Here's
a good example of its usage from Italian fashion designer Elsa
Schiaparelli (1890-1973) in her *Shocking Life*.

> Fashion is born by small facts, trends, or even politics,
> never by trying to make little pleats and furbelows, ...

---

furbelow, noun (**fur'** buh low)
A ruffle, flounce, or a pleated or gathered piece of material,
e.g. a flounce on a woman's dress.
A piece of showy ornamentation, or something that suggests
a furbelow in being showy or superfluous.
Can also be a verb – to decorate with a ruffle or flounce.
Likely from farbello, a Provençal word meaning fringe.

It's not unusual for furbelow to describe speech or writing, for
example, in this line by Sir Richard Steele (1672-1729):

> They ... expatiated in very florid harangues, ... and
> furbelow, if I may be allowed the metaphor, with many
> periodical sentences and turns of oratory.

I'm expatiating (elaborating) with the following furbelow:

furbelow

Furbelows. You'll find them places
Where you'll find pleats, puckers, laces:
  Frocks with fancy filigree;
  Flouncy, frilly finery;
Fringes, feathers, frothy froufrou –
Fashion's frivolous what-have-you!

Furbelow. Ornamentation.
Also found in speech, oration:
  Prose that's florid and ornate;
  Lofty phrases, heavyweight,
Fraught with rhetoric inflated;
Showy. Over-decorated! 2000

 equivoque

William Shakespeare (1564-1616) wrote in *Henry VI, Part II*:

Her words do show her wit incomparable.

Some would groan and dispute that our next word shows wit. Like furbelows and the jabot, it is considered by those misanthropes to be superfluous. Others consider it the highest form of wit. I'm talking about another word for pun.

In *Verbatim,* Vol. 12, No. 1, is the statement (itself a pun)
The pun is mightier than the word,
since it says more than one thing at a time, often producing a third meaning in the process, ...

That other, fancier word for pun is

---

equivoque, noun (**ĕk'** wuh vōk' or **eek'**) Also **equivoke.**
An equivocal or ambiguous word, phrase, or expression, and thus liable to more than one interpretation.
A pun; a double entendre; play on words; witticism.
From the French equivoque.

In *Cato's Letter No. 101,* actually written in 1722 by Sir John Trenchard (1661-1723), is the opinion:

There are so many Equivoques in Language, so many Sneers in Expression, which naturally carry one Meaning, and yet may intend another, that it is impossible by any fixed and stated Rules to determine the Intention, and punish all who deserve to be punished.

I hope I haven't committed any "Sneers in Expression" in the following verse. And I hope I don't deserve pun-ishment.

equivoque

Once u-pun an **equivoque**,

Bach and sons went for baroque;

Bad guys weren't in humankind;

Glaziers had a frame of mind;

There was pro- and anti-freeze;

Bailiffs carried minor keys;

Barbers took it on the chin;

Happy cows sang Lohengrin;

Chilly geese got human bumps;

Sugar daddies took their lumps;

Gambling gardeners hedged their bets;

Army bands had colonelettes;

Tailors took it off the cuff;

Shoes were polished in the buff;

Bakers got their just desserts;

Baby squid grew up in spurts;

Butchers were a cut above;

Tactful goats wore people gloves;

Higher learning? For giraffes;

Paunch lines made for belly laughs;

Eggheads didn't get the yolk,

(Once u-pun an **equivoque**.) 2003

diffident

This next verse, like it or not, also contains equivoques, or plays on words. Of course, you may be one of those having very strong views about puns. Or about other issues, for that matter.

But however strident your opinions, try to keep this little English proverb in mind when making your arguments:

> It is good to find modest words to express immodest things.

Confucius (551-479 BC), in *The Analects*, also spoke up for understatement:

> He who speaks without modesty will find it difficult to make his words good.

Here's a good, modest word:

---

diffident, adj. (**dĭf'** ih dŭnt)
Showing modest reserve. Reserved in manner; unassertive, restrained.
Lacking self-confidence. Timid, shy, self-effacing

Anthony Trollope's (1815-1882) *Barchester Towers* shows the word in context:

> 'Arabin is, in my opinion, the most free from any taint of self-conceit. His fault is that he's too diffident.

From a 2006 episode of the television series *The Gilmore Girls* is the question:

> I don't particularly like to take on such meek, diffident cases. Do you even know what diffident means?

We certainly do now!
And we can recite the following verse to prove it!

110

diffident

Dare to be **diffident**. Dare to defer.

Make "Unassertive" your motto.

Practice restraint and reserve, and prefer

Modesty over bravado.

Dare to be faltering, humble, and meek,

Hesitant, free from conceit.

Step to a rhythm that's halting and weak.

March to a **diffident** beat.   2000

career / careen

When there is a great ocean dividing us from a country that shares our language, we can grow apart over the meanings of words. Is one usage correct and the other flawed? Here's a suggestion from Henry David Thoreau (1817-1862) in *A Week on the Concord and Merrimack Rivers*:

> Where shall we look for standard English, but to the words of a standard man?

As you can probably tell from the title of this editorial, the writer has strong views about American versus British/Canadian usage:

> My own 1999 *Concise Oxford* tells me that the word "careen" can now be used as another word for "career"… "Yes, Language Does Evolve – Unfortunately," *The Gazette* (Montreal), April 24, 2006, A20.

---

career / careen, verbs (kŭ **reer'** / kŭ **reen'**)

career comes from a Latin word meaning course or route, and in English it originally meant to move or speed over a course. It still means to move forward at high speed. This meaning is standard in Britain, where a train might career off the rails, or a car career wildly off the road. In the United States, its use as a verb is rare. It has a whole different meaning and life as a noun.

careen began life meaning the keel of a ship, and to careen meant (and still means) to turn a ship on one side to work on its bottom. From this origin, it carries the additional meaning of sideways motion, rocking or wavering. For whatever reason, in American usage, it has been substituted for "career," and the latter has almost ceased to be used as a verb. Instead, careen has essentially taken over the meaning of running wild. Here, in the USA, trains and cars careen off the track or road. Purists still argue otherwise, however, and cling to the British usage.

Hang on tight. We're careering / careening to our next verse:

career / careen

It's rounding the corner at speeds very well
Exceeding those common to bats out of hell.
It's up on two wheels, wildly out of control,
Careening breakneck at full tilt – on a roll.

But way 'cross The Pond, going lickety-split,
Its counterpart whizzes, at speeds every bit
As rapid and rash. Yet when this auto veers …
It's British. It doesn't **careen**. It **careers**! 2006

bamboozle

Resistance to change is more the rule than the exception. Centuries haven't changed that truism. Witness this outburst from Jonathan Swift (1667-1745):

> The third refinement ... consists of the choice of certain words invented by some pretty fellows, such as banter, bamboozle, and kidney ... some of which are now struggling for the vogue, and others are in possession of it.

I'm not sure I'd call bamboozle in vogue, exactly. But I'm glad it hung in there, because it adds variety and gets its point across with a certain humor and light-heartedness.

---

bamboozle, verb (băm **boo'** zl)
To take in by elaborate means of deceit; to deceive by trickery; hoodwink. Delude, deceive, trick, cheat, swindle, victimize, defraud, gull, rook, gyp, mislead, fool.
Dates from the early 1700s. Orig. slang, perhaps Scottish, from bombaze (perplex). Also, perhaps related to bombast, or the French embabuiner, to make a fool (baboon) of.

Here are quotes from a couple of Swift's countrymen from later times, who seemed to have no problems with the word bamboozle:

> It is well known what a middleman he is: he is a man who bamboozles one party and plunders another.
> Benjamin Disraeli (1804-1881)

> Perhaps if I wanted to be understood or to understand I would bamboozle myself into belief, but I am a reporter ...
> Graham Greene (1904-1991)

Here's a verse to bamboozle you – in the best of ways:

114

bamboozle

What a dandy word: **bamboozle!**
(Notwithstanding Swift's refusal
to embrace it as legit.)

Used for dupe, deceive, or flim-flam,
Hoodwink, swindle, gull, or trick, **bamboozle** is a perfect fit! 1999

alack

Jonathan Swift was not the only person wielding a pen to deplore changes for the worse in language. In *The Literary Life,* Anatole France (1844-1924) reminisced:

> It was in the barbarous, gothic times when words had a meaning; in those days, writers expressed thoughts.

And Aubrey Beardsley (1872-1898) wrote in *The Story of Venus and Tannhauser, or Under the Hill*:

> In the present age, alas! Our pens are ravished by unlettered authors and unmannered critics, that make a havoc rather than a building, a wilderness rather than a garden. But, alack! What boots it to drop tears upon the preterit?

---

alack, interjection (uh **lăk'**)
A word used to express sorrow, regret, or alarm. Often used with alas.
From ah, lack, from lack in Middle English. A sense of loss, failure, reproach, shame.

Shakespeare used the word frequently, often without the obligatory alas. Here is an example from *A Midsummer Night's Dream*:

> What, out of hearing? gone? no sound, no word?
> Alack, where are you speak, an if you hear;

Sir Walter Scott wrote in *The Heart of Mid-Lothian*:

> Alack! alack! she never breathed word to me about it, …

Our final verse makes up for a lack of alack and echoes the sentiments of Anatole France and Aubrey Beardsley, expressed above:

alack

Oh, for those barb'rous, gothic times
Of magic prose and gloomy rhymes,
When words had meaning, and a thought
Was written clearly, as it ought.
Now, in our present age, alas!
Consider what has come to pass:
    Unlettered and unmannered men
    Create a havoc with the pen –
    A wilderness of ravished phrase,
    And barren works. Yes, nowadays,
    Your literary man, **alack**!
    Has all the markings of a hack.

(We've wept for, mourned, **alack**'d, alas'd
… the preterit, i.e. the past!) 2001

Dear reader,

We've been from A to Z. And back,
Alack.

Our book, and all good things, must pass,
Alas.

I hope you've had a pleasant read.
Godspeed.

Thanks for your company,

Susan Jones
(WORDS'WORTH©)

Quotation Attributions

Quotes from	. . . . . in
Peter Abrahams (b. 1919)	yesteryear
Abigail Adams (1744-1818)	vacillate
Noah Adams	mot juste
Zoë Akins (1886-1958)	Procrustean
Louisa May Alcott (1832-1888)	cockamamie
William Alexander (1826-1894)	ken
W. H. Auden (1907-1973)	mesomorph
Jane Austen (1775-1817)	disingenuous
Mary Hunter Austin (1868-1934)	susurrus
Nicholas Barber (*The Independent*)	rodomontade
Aubrey Beardsley (1872-1898)	alack
Robert Bresson (b. 1970)	mot juste
Jerry Brewer (*Seattle Times*)	jabot
Mark Broatch (*Sunday Star-Times*)	nimiety
August Brown (*Florida Times-Union*)	vapidity
Norman O. Brown (1913-2002)	flout
Thomas Alexander Browne (Rolf Boldrewood) (1826-1915)	lissome
Robert Browning (1812-1889)	zabaglione
John Bunyan (1628-1688)	lucubration
Samuel Butler (1612-1680)	trenchant
Lord Byron (1788-1824)	zephyr
	susurrus
Samuel Butler (1612-1680)	trenchant
Julius Caesar (100-44 BC)	yare
Guy Wetmore Carryl (1873-1904)	tuffet
Phoebe Cary (1824-1871)	trenchant
G. K. Chesterton (1874-1936)	hauteur
Winston Churchill (1875-1965)	eructation
Paul Claudel (1868-1955)	quotidian
Samuel Taylor Coleridge (1772-1834)	wroth
	Xanadu
Confucius (551-479 BC)	diffident
	trenchant
Charles Dickens (1812-1870)	rumination
Benjamin Disraeli (1804-1881)	bamboozle
Bob Dylan (b. 1941)	nonage
Tyron Edwards (1809-1894)	indolence
T. S. Eliot (1888-1965)	querulous

119

Ralph Waldo Emerson (1803-1882)	yare
Louise Erdrich	nimiety
Willard R. Espy (1910-1999)	Procrustean
John Evelyn (1620-1706)	eructation
Frederic William Farrar (1831-1903)	umbrageous
Gustave Flaubert (1821-1880)	vapidity
Ford Madox Ford (1873-1939)	mot juste
Anatole France (1844-1924)	alack
Johann Wolfgang von Goethe (1749-1832)	quotidian
Mary Gold (*Daily Mail*)	mesomorph
Martha Graham (1894-1991) – (*NYT* interview)	mesomorph
Graham Greene (1904-1991)	bamboozle
Agnes Kendrick Gray, (b.1894?)	ken
Thomas Gray (1716-1771)	zephyr
James Norman Hall (1887-1951) and	
Charles Nordhoff (1887-1949)	gallimaufry
Learned Hand (1872-1961)	xanthic
Ednah Proctor (Clarke) Hayes (c.1866-1956)	lissome
William Hazlitt (1778-1830)	indolence
O. Henry (1862-1910)	kith
George Herbert (1593-1633)	jabot
Sir Arthur Helps (1813-1875)	jeremiad
R. S. Hillyer	nonage
Eric Hoffer (1902-1983)	nonage
Oliver Wendell Holmes (1809-1894)	glabrous
Horace (65-8 BC)	querulous
Henry James (1843-1916)	umbrageous
William James (1842-1910)	pule
King James I of England (1566-1625)	Stygian
Samuel Johnson (1709-1784)	indolence
Ben Jonson (c. 1573-1637)	lucubration
Immanuel Kant (1724-1804)	nonage
James J. Kilpatrick (b.1920)	glabrous
	xanthic
Rudyard Kipling (1865-1936)	rodomontade
D. H. Lawrence (1885-1930)	ab ovo
Richard Lederer (b.1938)	lissome
Martin Legrand (1843-1882)	orotund
Sinclair Lewis (1885-1951)	hunky-dory
G. C. Lichtenberg (1742-1799)	vapidity
John Locke (1632-1704)	querulous
Henry Wadsworth Longfellow (1807-1882)	rodomontade
	susurrus
David Mallet (c. 1705-1765)	querulous

H. L. Mencken (1880-1956)	flout
George Meredith (1828-1909)	hunky-dory
Henry More (1614-1687)	eructation
Ogden Nash (1902-1971)	oleaginous
	kith
Charles Nordhoff (1887-1949) and	
James Norman Hall (1887-1951)	gallimaufry
Dorothy (Lady Temple) Osborne (1627-1695)	insouciance
Dorothy Parker (1893-1967)	disingenuous
Edgar Allan Poe (1809-1849)	Procrustean
François Rabelais (c. 1494-1553)	ken
Sir Walter Raleigh (c. 1552-1618)	yare
Eugen Rosenstock-Huessy (1888-1973)	ululate
Sir Walter Scott. (1771-1832)	insouciance
William Shakespeare (1564-1616)	hauteur
	indolence
	quotidian
	Stygian
	ululate
	quotidian
	rumination
	wroth
	wanton
	pule
	nimiety
	equivoque
	alack
Elsa Schiaparelli (1890-1973)	furbelow
Steven Sills	xanthic
John Simon (b. 1925)	ab ovo
Tobias Smollett (1721-1771)	eructation
Thomas Southern, (1660-1746)	brummagem
John Spencer (1630-1693)	quotidian
Sir Richard Steele (1672-1729)	furbelow
Jonathan Swift (1667-1745)	furbelow
	bamboozle
Alfred, Lord Tennyson (1809-1892)	vacillate
	tuffet
	jeremiad
William Makepeace Thackeray (1811-1863)	ab ovo
Henry David Thoreau (1817-1862)	career/careen
James Thurber (1894-1961)	jabot
Ellen Tien (*NYT*)	jabot
Sir John Trenchard (1661-1723)	equivoque

Anthony Trollope (1815-1882)	diffident
Mark Twain (1835-1910)	umbrageous
	orotund
Sir John Vanbrugh (1664-1726)	flout
François Villon (c. 1431-1463)	yesteryear
Voltaire (1694-1778)	ken
	vacillate
Alfred North Whitehead (1861-1947)	nonage
Walt Whitman (1819-1892)	eructation
	Xanadu
	gallimaufry
John Greenleaf Whittier (1807-1892)	kith
Bern Williams	indolence
John Wilson (1785-1854)	orotund
Simon Winchester	gallimaufry
In the Line of Fire (Movie)	cockamamie
Fanboys (Movie)	hunky-dory
Sweet Hostage (Movie)	Xanadu
The Gilmore Girls (TV Movie)	diffident
Home Improvement (TV Series)	ululate
Psalms 55:21	oleaginous
Psalms 19:14	rumination
Job 24:3	gallimaufry

Acknowledgments

I want to thank the following people for helping me prepare this book for publication. They gave of their valuable time to read, aid, abet, encourage, and make suggestions. I owe them more than I can say. I've listed them alphabetically.

Thank you for your support, editorial expertise, extraordinary friendship, time, love, and patience.

Helen Anderson
Judith Bohlen
Leslie Brockman
Cathy Jones
Jeff Jones
Bob Jones
William Jones
Suzanne Maricich
Sally Montgomery
Michael Stugrin (Power-by-Words.com)
Kevin and Laura Weed

Also, many thanks to Charlene Whitney Edwards (www.wedesign.com) for her brilliant and imaginative cover artwork.

Thanks, too, to **Judith C. R**eveal (**J**ust**C**reativew**R**iting.com) for her uplifting words and her excellent professional editing services.

For words, like nature, half reveal
And half conceal the soul within.

Alfred, Lord Tennyson (1809-1892)

WORDS'WORTH©

(Susan Jones) was born in Oregon and grew up at the end of a canyon, in a setting homesteaded by her Swedish bachelor immigrant great uncle.

Trips back and forth to Portland for music lessons rounded out a life filled with school, family, friends, and church. Contests, recitals, youth orchestra, summers at Aspen and Tanglewood – all punctuated her years at college, where she earned a degree in German.

Then came marriage, children, and a career teaching and performing professionally in Portland. In 1980, an odyssey eastward began, to Minneapolis, Indianapolis, and finally DC. It was in Indiana that Susan earned a Masters Degree in Library Science, then found herself managing a corporate library. There, her colleagues asked her to begin the word-of-the-week service that developed into WORDS'WORTH.

Perhaps it was her father's relish in reciting his repertoire of verse, such as "The Walrus and the Carpenter," "The Deacon's Masterpiece," "The Antiseptic Baby and the Prophylactic Pup," "Casey at Bat." Perhaps it was soaking in Lutheran hymns. Or playing the piano and clarinet. Words, verse, melody, and rhythm jelled into WORDS'WORTH.

For several years, Susan divided her time between life in DC (still a corporate librarian) and writing verse on an island in the Chesapeake Bay.

Then, unplanned events prompted a move back to the West Coast, and she spent four years in Orange County, California. Can you spell ricochet? WORDS'WORTH is now back on her Eastern Shore island and continuing the California connection by living much of her life in Long Beach.

125

How could the poet
possibly know
till the very last word
in the very last row?
Richard Armour (1906-1989)

Order information

Here's how to order more copies of this book for your friends, colleagues, kith, and kin – in short, **everyone** in your circle of acquaintances who would love an entertaining, amusing, instructive, and per-verse romp through the alphabet:

- Fetch your credit card.
- Type or copy/paste in your browser – www.amazon.com.
- Order several. (Think of your gift list!)

What could be simpler!

Also, check out the following web pages:

- www.wordsworthverse.com – (Always a featured word!)
- www.whimsypublishing.com – (What's in the pipeline?)

Order information

Here's how to order more copies of this book for your friends, colleagues, kith, and kin – in short, **everyone** in your circle of acquaintances who would love an entertaining, amusing, instructive, and per-verse romp through the alphabet:

- Fetch your credit card.
- Type or copy/paste in your browser – www.amazon.com.
- Order several. (Think of your gift list!)

What could be simpler!

Also, check out the following web pages:
- www.wordsworthverse.com – (Always a featured word!)
- www.whimsypublishing.com – (What's in the pipeline?)